BR 9/91

Mills College Childrens School

DEMCO

KOREANS

**Mugunghwa
(hibiscus)
Korea's national flower**

IMMIGRATION
AND THE
AMERICAN WAY OF LIFE

Geologically speaking, the continent of North America is very old. The people who live here, by comparison, are new arrivals. Even the first settlers, the American Indians who came here from Asia about 35,000 years ago, are fairly new, not to speak of the first European settlers who came by ship or the refugees who flew in yesterday. Whenever they came, they were all immigrants. How all these immigrants live together today to form one society has been compared to the making of a mosaic. A mosaic is a picture formed from many different pieces. Thus, in America, many groups of people—from African Americans or Albanians to Tibetans or Welsh—live side by side. This human mosaic was put together by the immigrants themselves, with courage, hard work, and luck. Each group of immigrants has its own history and its own reasons for coming to America. Immigrants from different regions have their own way of creating communities for themselves and their children. In creating those communities, they not only keep elements of their own heritage alive but also enrich further the fabric of American society. Each book in *Recent American Immigrants* will examine a part of this human mosaic up close. The books will look at some of the most recent arrivals to find out what they are like and how they fit into the whole mosaic.

Recent American Immigrants

KOREANS

Jodine Mayberry

Consultant
Roger Daniels, Department of History
University of Cincinnati

Franklin Watts
New York • London • Toronto • Sydney

Developed by: Ω **Visual Education Corporation**
Princeton, NJ

Maps: Patricia R. Isaacs/Parrot Graphics

Cover photograph: Tony Freeman/PhotoEdit

Photo Credits: p. 3 (L) Van Bucher/Photo Researchers, Inc.; p. 3 (M)
Janet Wishnetsky/Comstock; p. 3 (R) Lawrence Migdale; p. 8 Korea
National Tourism Corporation; p. 14 Hawaii State Archives; p. 16
Bishop Museum; p. 20 Mary Paik Lee/Sucheng Chan; p. 21 Pacific
Photo Gallery/Bishop Museum; p. 22 Courtesy of Susan Ahn Cuddy; p.
24 Library of Congress; p. 27 Courtesy of Young OK Chung; p. 29 (L)
John Colwell/Grant Heilman; p. 29 (R) Grant Heilman; p. 35 Mel
Digiacomo/The Image Bank; p. 36 Chuck Fishman/Woodfin Camp &
Associates, Inc.; p. 39 Lawrence Migdale; p. 40 Lawrence Migdale; p.
42 Chuck Fishman/Woodfin Camp & Associates, Inc.; p. 45 Michael
Hirsch/Gamma-Liaison; p. 46 David R. Frazier Photolibrary; p. 49
Lawrence Migdale; p. 51 Courtesy of the Philip Jaisohn Memorial
Center; p. 52 UPI/Bettmann; p. 53 UPI/Bettmann; p. 54 UPI/
Bettmann; p. 55 Janet Wishnetsky/Comstock; p. 56 Janet Wishnetsky/
Comstock; p. 59 Alain Evrard/Photo Researchers, Inc.;
p. 61 Lawrence Migdale.

Library of Congress Cataloging-in-Publication Data

Mayberry, Jodine
Koreans / Jodine Mayberry.
p.   cm. — (Recent American Immigrants)
Includes bibliographical references and index.
Summary: Portrays the life-styles of this hard-working and successful
group of new Americans, and shows how they have adjusted to their
new home while preserving many of their old customs.
ISBN 0-531-11106-7
1. Korean Americans — Juvenile literature. 2. United States —
Emigration and immigration — Juvenile literature. 3. Korea —
Emigration and immigration — Juvenile literature. [1. Korean
Americans. 2. United States — Emigration and immigration.]
I. Title. II. Series.
E184.K6M29   1991
305.8957073 — dc20   90-12987 CIP AC

Contents

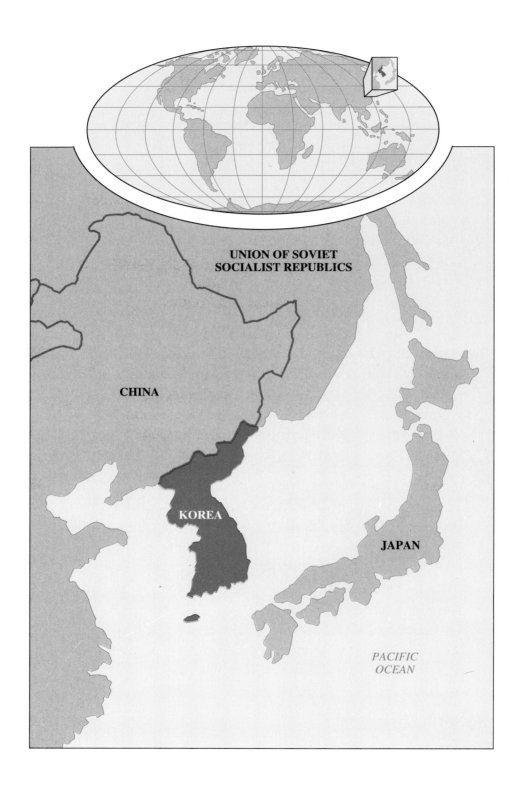

UNION OF SOVIET
SOCIALIST REPUBLICS

CHINA

KOREA

JAPAN

PACIFIC
OCEAN

Early Korean Immigration

Korea is a beautiful, mountainous land. Its name means "land of the morning calm." It is located on a peninsula between the Yellow Sea and the Sea of Japan. China lies to the north and west. Japan lies to the east and south, as close as about 125 miles south across the Korea Strait.

KOREA: A BRIEF HISTORY

Over the centuries, Korea was invaded many times. It was heavily influenced by the Chinese, Japanese, and other Asian peoples. Nevertheless, Koreans have had their own distinct civilization for thousands of years. Ancient Korean tribes built walled towns. Eventually, groups of towns joined together to form three kingdoms. These kingdoms had their own laws, government, and culture. Ancient Korean artisans produced beautiful bronze and gold statues and ornaments. They also made fine porcelains and paintings. They produced moveable metal type two hundred years ahead of the Europeans.

For centuries, most Koreans were farmers. They raised rice, wheat, fruits, and vegetables. Over time, Koreans adopted the ideas of Confucianism from China and Buddhism from India.

For centuries, Koreans have been harvesting wheat in settings like this one.

The Hermit Kingdom   China dominated Korea for 300 years from the late 1500s to the late 1800s. During that period, only a few Korean scholars and students traveled outside of the country. Even then, they went only as far as China or Japan to study. Korea remained so isolated from the rest of the world that it was nicknamed the "Hermit Kingdom."

Conflict Over Korea   A hundred years ago, Korea was a weak nation, unable to remain free of its powerful neighbors. China, Russia, and Japan became rivals over Korea. Each nation wanted to control the Korean Peninsula. Gradually,

Japan won out. Japan and China fought a war in Korea from 1894 to 1895. The Japanese won the war and occupied Korea. From 1904 to 1905 Japan fought with Russia over territory in China and Korea. Japan also won that war and strengthened its hold over Korea. In 1905, Japan made Korea a "protectorate." This meant that Japan directed Korea's relations with other nations. Finally, in 1910, Japan "annexed" Korea. In effect, Japan simply took possession of Korea and made it a colony of the Japanese empire.

The Korean people hated their Japanese rulers. The Japanese took their lands away from them. Many Koreans were forced to move to other parts of the country to work for Japanese companies. Thousands of Koreans were thrown in jail, tortured, or killed. Japan also tried to destroy Korean culture. They destroyed Korean history books and forced Korean children to learn the Japanese language in school.

Korea remained a Japanese colony until the United States defeated Japan in 1945. All during those years Koreans longed for their own independent nation. Many Koreans fled their Japanese rulers and settled in the Soviet Union, China, and the United States. Wherever they went, they kept their dream of a free country alive.

KOREANS COME TO AMERICA

Japan was not the only nation to gain entry to the Hermit Kingdom. In 1882, Korea entered into a treaty of friendship and trade with the United States. This treaty was called the Treaty of Chemulpo. It allowed the United States to send diplomats, merchants, and Christian missionaries to Korea. It also permitted Koreans to travel to the United States.

The first Christian missionaries arrived in Korea in 1885. They were both Protestants and Catholics. They succeeded in converting thousands of Koreans to Christianity. The missionaries printed Bibles in the Korean language. They also started schools that taught Western languages, culture, and medicine. They taught the Korean converts about the history and government of Western nations.

Korean Students and Refugees   The missionaries inspired many Koreans to leave their own shores and go out into the wider world. To many Korean Christians, America was the center of their religion. It was also a place where Koreans could go to get an education. The first Koreans to go to America were Christian students. In 1883, Korea sent a diplomatic mission to the United States. One of the members of the mission remained in America to go to school. Three more students came in 1885. One of those men was So Jae P'il. So became a medical doctor and Americanized his name to Philip Jaisohn. While the other two men who arrived with Jaisohn soon returned home, Jaisohn spent most of the rest of his life in America.

Between 1890 and 1905, several dozen Korean missionary students came to the United States. Most wanted to become doctors or ministers. There were no universities in Korea to train them for these vocations. In most cases, the students returned to Korea when they completed their educations.

Some of the students, however, were political refugees. They had participated earlier in an unsuccessful attempt to overthrow the Korean government in 1884. Three student refugees—Syngman Rhee, Ahn Chang-ho, and Pak Yong-man—became the leaders of a movement in America to free Korea from Japan. They remained in the United States for several years.

Immigration of Farm Laborers to Hawaii   The first large numbers of Korean Americans to immigrate to the United States were farm laborers who went to Hawaii to work in the sugarcane fields. In 1900 Hawaii was an American territory. It did not become a state until 1959. Hawaii's main industry was growing sugarcane. The growers, the Hawaiian Sugar Planters' Association (HSPA), needed thousands of laborers who would be willing to work hard for low wages. The planters went to foreign countries to hire laborers. At first, the HSPA recruited workers from China and Japan. Then they turned to Korea and the Philippines for new laborers.

In Korea, the HSPA hired an American businessman, David Deshler, to recruit and transport workers to Hawaii. Deshler set up a bank in Korea that lent Korean workers the money they needed to book passage to Hawaii. The workers had to promise to work on the sugarcane plantations until they repaid the loans. Korean officials favored Korean immigration to America. They could bring in revenue by charging the emigrants $1 each for passports.

On January 13, 1903, 102 Korean immigrants arrived in Honolulu, Hawaii, aboard the SS *Gaelic*. Within two years, more than 7,000 other Koreans would arrive in Hawaii to work on the sugarcane plantations.

Horace Allen was the U.S. Minister to Korea. Here is how he described the Korean people in a report to the U.S. State Department in 1902:

> *Lately Koreans have become interested in the Hawaiian Islands where large numbers of Chinese and Japanese reside, and considerable numbers have desired to go to the islands with the hope of bettering their condition and escaping the persistent oppression of their tax collectors. The idea of obtaining an education for their children seems to be an incentive as well.*
>
> Source: As quoted in H. Brett Melendy, *Asians in America: Filipinos, Koreans, and East Indians* (Boston: Twayne, 1977), p. 124.

WHY THE KOREANS CAME

Earning a living was only one of many reasons why Koreans began to immigrate to Hawaii in 1903. A severe drought and famine in Korea the previous year had caused starvation among the Korean people. "We left Korea because we were too poor," wrote one immigrant. "We had nothing to eat. There was absolutely no way we could survive."[1]

In addition, Japan's wars with China and Russia and its occupation of Korea uprooted many Koreans and forced them to flee their homeland. The missionaries encouraged their Christian students to go to America and set up organizations to fight for Korean independence. The missionaries told them that America was a land of freedom and opportunity. It was also a land where their children could obtain good educations. For Koreans, as for all emigrant groups at that time, America was the place to come.

IMMIGRANTS AND EXILES IN HAWAII

When the Koreans arrived in Hawaii, they found thousands of Chinese and Japanese already working in the sugarcane fields. Most of the Chinese and Japanese workers were unmarried men or men who had left their families behind to come to America. They planned to work for a few years and return home as rich men. In the end, most of them never did go home again.

The Koreans differed from these earlier Asian immigrants in several ways. Of the approximately 7,000 Koreans who went to Hawaii between 1903 and 1905, about 700 were women. These were the wives of Korean immigrants who had brought their families with them. They intended to stay permanently. Many of the others were political refugees. They were exiles

[1] *Source:* As quoted in Ronald Takaki, *Strangers from a Different Shore: A History of Asian Americans* (Boston: Little, Brown, 1989), p. 55.

who believed they could not go home again until Korea freed itself from Japan.

Most of the Japanese and Chinese immigrants were peasants who had been farmers back home. In addition, most of them came from a specific region of China or Japan. The Koreans came from all walks of life. Some had been civil servants, clerks, or soldiers. Many came from cities. They came from all over the country, not from one particular region.

At least 40 percent of the Korean immigrants who went to Hawaii could read and write. As many as one-third had already become Christians before they left Korea. All these factors helped the Korean Americans adapt very quickly to their new land.

Here is what one Korean American wrote about the Korean immigrants and their adopted Hawaiian home:

> *The Koreans . . . are very emphatic in their statements that Hawaii is their home. They point with pride to their children who are becoming American citizens. They insist that here they have found what has made many of them happy and contented. . . . They say, "Here we have lived and here we will die. To us, more than any other race, is the name 'Paradise of the Pacific' a reality."*
> *Lee Tai Sung, 1932*
>
> Source: As quoted in Kim Hyung-Chan, *Dictionary of Asian American History* (New York: Greenwood, 1986), p. 108.

LIFE ON THE SUGARCANE PLANTATIONS

Hawaii was no paradise for the first Korean immigrants. Work in the sugarcane fields was dirty and hard. The workers had to get up at 5 A.M. and labor all day long in the hot sun. On most

**Korean workers on a Hawaiian sugarcane
plantation, around 1910**

plantations, they worked in gangs. Usually each gang was made up of a separate ethnic group—Japanese, Chinese, Korean, or Filipino.

The gangs walked or rode trucks or trains out to the fields. In the fields, they were supervised by foremen called *lunas*, who were often Spanish or Portuguese. The lunas would not allow the workers to talk to each other. If workers talked or fell behind, the luna would whip them.

The work itself was backbreaking. The field hands had to bend over to hoe the rows of sugarcane for four hours at a time before resting. At harvest time, they swung big knives called *machetes* to cut and bundle the sugarcane stalks. To protect themselves from the sharp leaves of the sugarcane, they had to wear heavy clothing and gloves even in the heat. Nevertheless, their hands and arms usually bled from dozens of cuts by the end of the day.

One of the worst things about toiling in the sugarcane fields was the *bango*. Bangos were brass disks engraved with identification numbers. The workers wore them on chains around their necks. The lunas never called the laborers by anything but their bango numbers. They were not even granted the dignity of being called by their names.

The Korean workers received about $16 per week, plus free housing and medical care. However, food and other expenses came to about $6 to $10 per week. This made it difficult for the Koreans to save money to repay their fares.

The Work Camps   The work camps varied from plantation to plantation. Most were crowded and dirty with no running water or sanitation. The workers on each plantation were usually divided by ethnic group and housed in separate camps. Many camps took in 200 to 300 people. Most workers lived in barracks. Those with families were usually given small rooms, one room to a family. After working in the fields all day, the laborers would have to wait their turn for the camp's one bathtub.

Some women did the same work as the men in the fields. The women, however, received less money than the men for the same jobs. Most women did not work in the fields. Instead, they cooked, packed meals for the men, and washed clothes for their families and the other workers.

Life in the camps was not all misery. Most camps had bands, baseball teams, and churches. Some workers took great pains to clean and decorate their camps.

Korean work camp at Ewa Plantation, Oahu, 1925.
This camp was well maintained over the years.

Ethnic Division on the Plantations   By 1903, more than 20,000 Japanese had come to work on the sugar plantations. They made up more than two-thirds of the plantations' work force. The planters felt the Japanese had become too numerous. They wanted to bring in workers from other countries to counterbalance the Japanese. The planters were particularly glad to recruit Korean workers. They knew the Koreans hated the Japanese.

The planters used a "divide-and-conquer" system for keeping the workers from joining forces. They paid different ethnic groups different wages. They kept the workers in separate work gangs and camps. They also pitted different ethnic groups against each other in the fields. For example, a luna might tell a gang of Koreans that they were not working as hard as the Filipinos or Japanese. This would hurt the Koreans' pride and cause them to work harder.

The divide-and-conquer system worked very well for decades. Until the 1920s, each ethnic group in Hawaii had its own labor union called a "blood union." When one union went on strike, the other unions allowed their members to be used as strikebreakers. When the Japanese blood unions struck, the planters knew they could count on Korean workers to cross the picket lines. In 1920, when Japanese American union members went on a long strike against the planters, the other blood unions joined them. But more than 100 Koreans volunteered to break the strike. "We don't wish to be looked upon as strikebreakers, but we shall continue to work . . ." announced the Korean Americans. "We are opposed to the Japanese in everything."[1] After that strike, the blood unions learned to work together instead of undermining each other.

---

[1] *Source:* As quoted in Ronald Takaki, *Strangers from a Different Shore: A History of Asian Americans* (Boston: Little, Brown, 1989), p. 154.

THE GENTLEMEN'S AGREEMENT

The Korean immigration to Hawaii lasted only two years. In 1905, the Japanese government halted Korean immigration to the islands. Japanese immigrants in Hawaii had pressured the Japanese government to stop the flow. They did not want the planters to use the Koreans against them.

At that time, many Americans did not want any more Japanese or Koreans to come to the United States. They believed the Asians were taking jobs away from Americans. In 1905, labor unions in San Francisco started the Japanese and Korean Exclusion League. This organization sought to keep all Japanese and Koreans—later all Asians—out of the United States.

In 1907–08, Japan voluntarily agreed to halt the immigration of all Japanese and Korean workers to the United States. This was called the "Gentlemen's Agreement." It was intended to prevent the U.S. Congress from passing a law to exclude all Japanese and Koreans from the United States.

Under the terms of the agreement, only students and the wives, children, and parents of those already residing in the United States could immigrate to America. Workers who had gone back to Japan or Korea leaving family or property in the United States could also return. Later anti-Asian U.S. legislation in 1917 and 1924 all but stopped Japanese and Korean immigration.

Thus only a few hundred Koreans were allowed to immigrate to the United States from 1907 until 1952. Most of those who did emigrate from Korea were wives, students, and a few political refugees. The Korean population of the United States remained very stable. Most were in Hawaii, where between 1920 and 1940 the population increased from 4,950 to only 6,851. Most of that increase was due to births, not immigration.

EARLY ORGANIZATIONS

In order to succeed in America, most immigrants formed groups or organizations to help each other adapt to their new land. Some organizations were based on family ties. Some people formed groups with immigrants who had come from the same villages or regions in their homelands. Korean Americans, however, did not form groups based on families, villages, or regions back home. Their organizations were based on governmental, social, and religious needs in their new homeland.

Tonghoe   Whenever a Hawaiian work camp housed more than ten Korean families, the families formed a *tonghoe*, or "village council." The adult males elected a village chief, called a *tongiang*, who headed the village council. The tongiang was elected once a year. The purpose of the village council was to maintain order and enforce the law. The council was empowered to arrest, try, and punish wrongdoers. The usual punishment was a fine or flogging. A member of the village might be punished for drunkenness or gambling, for example. The fines were placed in a community fund to help the members of the village.

Sworn Brotherhoods   Some Koreans also formed secret societies called "sworn brotherhoods." The secret societies were intended to protect Koreans from violence from outsiders. Sometimes the brotherhoods became rivals with one another and caused trouble within the Korean community.

Women's Associations   Many Korean women belonged to women's associations. These groups worked to preserve Korean language and culture in America. The group members provided friendship, help, and comfort to one another. One of the first women's associations was formed in San Francisco in 1908.

THE ROLE OF THE CHURCH

The most important organizations among the early Korean immigrants were their Christian churches. Korean immigrants held their first church service in Hawaii in 1903. They established their first church on the mainland, the Korean Methodist Church of San Francisco, in 1905.

The plantation owners allowed the Koreans to have one or more churches at each work camp. The churches became the center of camp life. It was there that weddings, funerals, baptisms, and parties took place.

Many Korean churches offered Korean language classes to Korean children. The Korean immigrants sent their children to public schools because they wanted them to get a good education. At the same time, they did not want them to forget the language and culture of their homeland. The church-run language schools taught not only the language but also the history, geography, and culture of Korea.

Korean workers at church, Ewa Plantation, Oahu, 1905

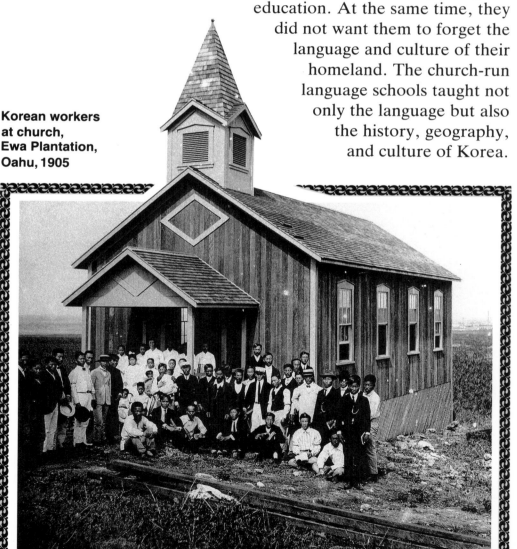

Korean students at Kawaiahao Seminary in Hawaii, 1908

EXILE POLITICS

Most, if not all, of the Koreans who came to Hawaii and later to the U.S. mainland considered themselves as *yumin,* or "exiles," from their homeland. They felt a keen sense of loss. They were people without a country. As stated earlier, they believed that they could not go home until their land was freed from the hated Japanese. In the meantime, they tried to preserve their culture and language in America. This gave them a deep sense of purpose. They spoke Korean at home and sent their children to Korean language schools. They attended independence meetings and observed Korean national holidays.

Almost immediately upon arriving in Hawaii, the Korean Americans began to form organizations to work for Korea's independence. Koreans in Honolulu started the New People's Society in 1903. By 1907, at least twenty additional political organizations had sprung up in Hawaii. Two of these organizations merged and formed the Korean National Association (KNA) in 1909. The KNA became one of the largest and most powerful Korean organizations in America.

These nationalist groups provided money to support resistance groups back in Korea. In 1918, Korean rice farmers in California donated more than $42,000 to resistance organizations in Korea. They also lobbied the U.S. government to support Korean nationalism.

The Korean American churches were also hotbeds of political activity. The churches sponsored debates on such topics as "the duty of Koreans abroad." The church-run language and culture classes also taught about Korean nationalism. This combination of religion and politics helped to unite the small and scattered Korean American community.

THREE LEADERS IN KOREAN AMERICAN POLITICS

The struggle for Korean independence went on year after year for more than forty years. During that time, differences arose over how best to achieve independence. People became divided into three main factions. Each faction was led by one of three Korean Americans: Syngman Rhee, Ahn Chang-ho, and Pak Yong-man.

Syngman Rhee (1875–1965) was the most important of the three leaders, in part because he was the only one who lived to see Korea made free. He believed that the way to secure Korean independence was through political pressure. He wanted the world's most powerful nations to force Japan to give up Korea.

Pak Yong-man (1881–1928) believed the only way to free Korea was to raise an army to fight Japan. He tried to train Korean American students to become soldiers. Ahn Chang-ho (1878–1938) believed that Korea would be freed only after a long struggle. He argued that the movement should develop an elite new generation of leaders.

Ahn Chang-ho

MOVING TO THE CITY

Most Korean immigrants soon abandoned the sugarcane fields to seek a better life in Hawaii's cities. Some left the plantations as soon as they repaid their passage to Hawaii. By 1910, about 10 percent of the Korean immigrants had moved to either Honolulu or Hilo, Hawaii's two largest cities. Little by little, other plantation workers followed, until in 1930 only 484 Koreans remained on the plantations.

Some city dwellers went to work for the Dole pineapple factory in Honolulu. Others worked on pineapple and macadamia nut plantations. Some started their own farms or flower gardens. A few Korean Americans opened small businesses such as restaurants, grocery stores, and boardinghouses.

While they remained isolated on the plantations, Korean Americans were able to preserve their culture. Once they moved to the cities, however, many lost their sense of ethnic identity. As people without a homeland, they were resigned to living the rest of their lives in America. Many Korean men married women from other ethnic groups because there was a shortage of Korean women in Hawaii. These multiethnic families discarded old traditions and adopted new ones as they made new lives for themselves in Hawaii.

Like most immigrant children, young Koreans adapted even faster than their parents to American life. Despite the Korean language schools, the children quickly became Americans in language, dress, activities, and ideas. They made friends outside of their ethnic group, even with the children of Japanese immigrants. They had not lived under Japanese rule and saw no point in hating Japanese Americans.

Moving to the Mainland, 1905–1965

Most Koreans were discouraged by the hard life on the sugar plantations. The work was much more difficult than they had expected. Furthermore, it did not make them as rich or even comfortably well off as they had hoped. Between 1905 and 1907, several hundred disappointed Koreans returned to their homeland. Other Koreans moved to the American mainland. Even though they had not realized their dreams in Hawaii, they still believed that America was the place to be.

The majority of these Koreans went first to San Francisco (opposite) and then settled in California. Some went to Arizona to build railroads. Others went to Montana, Utah, Wyoming, or Colorado to work in the copper or coal mines. Other Koreans went to Alaska to work in fish canneries. Like other Asian immigrants, some Koreans had to take menial, low-paying jobs as house servants, gardeners, janitors, and waiters.

Most of those who settled in California became migrant farm workers. Some Korean Americans were able to lease or buy their own land and become independent farmers. They raised rice or planted fruit trees. They ran small family farms of ten to eighty acres.

SCATTERED IMMIGRANTS

Most of the 1,015 Korean Americans who moved to the mainland from Hawaii between 1905 and 1910 were men. Only 45 were women and 29 were children. The rest were unmarried men or men who had left wives in Korea. They were able to migrate again because they did not have families to tie them down. Some men sent back to Korea for brides after they reimmigrated. However, there were relatively few Korean women in the United States until the 1950s. In 1930, two-thirds of the Koreans in the United States were male.

Koreans also came in much smaller numbers than most other immigrant groups. In most places, there were too few Koreans to form a neighborhood or community. The Chinese and Japanese settled together in cities and formed "Chinatowns" and "Japan towns," but there were not enough Koreans to form "Korea towns." The Koreans usually had to find housing in the poorest sections. This often meant living in the Mexican quarter or in Chinatown.

Many of the Koreans who remained in California settled in the Los Angeles area. Some started small businesses such as restaurants and grocery stores. By the 1930s, Korean Americans operated more than sixty businesses in Los Angeles. These included trucking companies, hat shops, and herbal stores. Most of the businesses catered to Koreans and other Asian Americans.

Some Koreans were able to form a community of sorts. Farm hands and railroad workers usually lived and worked together. This enabled them to speak their own language, eat their own foods, and ease their loneliness with songs and stories from their homeland. The courage of these Koreans was remarkable. Like so many immigrants, they had to overcome incredible hardship before they felt at home in America.

LIFE AS A FARM WORKER

Korean farm hands usually worked in gangs of ten men. Each gang was supervised by a foreman called a *sip-chang*, which meant "ten-head," or that he had ten men under him. The gangs traveled around from farm to farm in the San Joaquin and Sacramento valleys of California. They picked peaches, plums, walnuts, lemons, and oranges. The Korean immigrants took great pride in their tasks. They believed that if they worked hard, their employers would want to hire more Koreans. That would enable all Korean Americans to have jobs. The farm hands had to stoop over all day in the hot sun. At the end of the day, they returned to their camps, where they bathed and ate and rested up for the next day. In some cases, there were no camps. The workers had to build their own shacks, or they slept in the fields or orchards.

A Korean American family, around 1920

DOUBLE DISCRIMINATION

Koreans in America tried very hard to adapt to Western culture. They wore American clothes, learned English, and worked very hard. They thought that if they did these things, white Americans would like them. But most whites failed to see any distinction between the Koreans and other Asians.

Like other Asian immigrants, Korean Americans suffered a great deal of discrimination. They could not eat in many restaurants or stay in most hotels. They could not live in white neighborhoods. They had to sit in separate sections of theaters along with Mexican Americans and blacks. They could not use public swimming pools and many beaches. Often, they were greeted by signs that announced, "Whites Only."

Koreans felt they were doubly discriminated against because whites constantly mistook them for Japanese. Many whites had never heard of Korea and did not know who Koreans were. Sometimes Koreans were denied jobs, chased out of town, and even beaten by people who thought they were Japanese. This treatment infuriated the Koreans who still hated the Japanese for conquering their homeland.

Some states passed laws that discriminated against Asians and other nonwhites. California enacted the Alien Land Act in 1913. This law prohibited noncitizens from buying land. Many other states soon passed similar laws. Koreans and others got around this law by purchasing land in the names of their American-born children who were citizens. In most western states, it was even illegal for a nonwhite to marry a white person. None of these laws exists any longer.

EARLY ENTREPRENEURS

Few whites would offer good jobs to Koreans or other Asians. Asian immigrants could, however, start their own small businesses, and many did. Some Korean Americans banded together and formed corporations to purchase large farms.

A few Koreans started rice farms in California. One, Kim Chong-nim, was so successful that he owned more than 2,000 acres of rice paddies by 1917. He was called the "Rice King" of California. Other Korean American companies purchased orchards and raised citrus fruit. The most successful Korean-owned orchard belonged to Charles Kim (Kim Ho) and Harry Kim (Kim Hyung-soon). They were unrelated but called their orchard the Kim Brothers Company. Eventually they owned six farms totaling 500 acres. The Kims are most famous for developing fuzzless peaches called "nectarines." The Kims donated $500,000 worth of real estate to set up the Korean Foundation in 1957.

A nectarine orchard in California. The nectarine was first developed by the Kim Brothers Company.

FIGHTING FOR CITIZENSHIP

Throughout the 1920s and 1930s, the number of Koreans in America remained very small. According to the U.S. Census Bureau, there were 6,181 Koreans in the United States in 1920 and only 8,568 by 1940. The Immigration Act of 1924 severely restricted the immigration of Asians. It had very little effect on Koreans, however, since the Japanese already prevented Koreans from immigrating to the United States.

The Immigration Act of 1924 also prevented Asian Americans from becoming citizens. This was very disappointing to thousands of Korean Americans. Most of them had spent most of their lives in the United States and considered it their home. But children who were born in America of Korean immigrants automatically became citizens because of the Fourteenth Amendment to the Constitution.

Mary Paik Lee is a Korean American who came to the United States in 1910, when she was five years old. She talks about citizenship in her autobiography, *Quiet Odyssey: A Pioneer Korean Woman in America:*

> *Once an American lady friend asked me if I was going to vote. I said I was too busy and couldn't get away. She started to give me a lecture about my civic duty. . . . She didn't know that the reason I didn't vote was that Orientals were not allowed to become citizens, so we didn't have the right to vote. She became very angry and said, "That's not so! Everyone in America has equal rights." But she came back a few days later and said a lawyer friend had told her that I was right. We remained good friends anyway.*
>
> Source: As quoted in Mary Paik Lee, *Quiet Odyssey: A Pioneer Korean Woman in America* (Seattle: Univ. of Washington Press, 1990), pp. 104–105.

THE GREAT DEPRESSION

Little is known about how Korean Americans fared during the Great Depression of the 1930s. With millions of people out of work, other Americans were very bitter about having to compete with Chinese, Japanese, and Mexican workers. Presumably Koreans, still lumped in with Japanese and Chinese, came in for their share of resentment. Like the Joad family, described so vividly in John Steinbeck's novel *The Grapes of Wrath*, thousands of bankrupt farmers and their families poured into California looking for farm work. There were not enough jobs for that many workers. As a result, some Korean migrant farm workers suffered from unemployment and poverty, as did other migrant workers. Korean Americans who had their own farms survived reasonably well during the depression. Some Korean American farmers were able to hire Korean migrant workers for planting and harvesting during this period.

WORLD WAR II

Japan attacked Pearl Harbor, Hawaii, on December 7, 1941. This surprise attack brought the United States into World War II. Korean Americans were very glad that the United States was at war with Germany and Japan. They hoped that the United States would defeat Japan and free their country from Japanese rule.

But the war also brought with it renewed discrimination against the Korean Americans. Both the American government and many other Americans failed to distinguish between Japanese and Koreans. The American government considered Korean Americans as Japanese "nationals" because Japan had annexed their country. This deeply offended the Korean Americans. "No one hates the Japanese more than we do," they would say.

"I Am Korean"   In Hawaii, Koreans were classified as enemy aliens. Those working on defense projects were made to wear badges with black borders identifying them as Japanese. When many Korean workers protested, they were allowed to print "I am Korean" on their badges. Often, when white Americans saw Koreans on the street, they assumed they were Japanese. Some people physically attacked Korean Americans because they thought them to be Japanese.

Individual Koreans enlisted in the military to fight the Japanese, but there were too few Korean Americans to organize any all-Korean units. Many enlistees were used as language teachers and translators because they knew the Japanese language. In Los Angeles, 109 Koreans joined the California Home Guard. They were placed in a special all-Korean unit, the Tiger Brigade. The brigade's job was to defend California against Japanese invasion. Korean Americans also served in the Red Cross and supported the war effort in many other ways.

KOREAN INDEPENDENCE AT LAST

As Korean Americans had hoped, the United States did defeat Japan in World War II and freed Korea. Korea became an independent republic in 1948. Syngman Rhee returned to Korea after more than forty years in the United States. He was soon elected the first president of the new nation. However, after the war, Korea was occupied by American troops in the south and Soviet troops in the north. The Soviets quickly set up a Communist government in the north.

In 1950, North Korea invaded South Korea. The United Nations sent troops, most of them American, to help South Korea fight North Korea. The Korean War lasted three years. Hundreds of thousands of soldiers and civilians, including 50,000 Americans, were killed before the war ended in a stalemate. North Korea and South Korea remain two separate, hostile nations, as shown in the map below.

The war had an enormous impact on Korean Americans. Most Korean Americans had relatives back home who were killed or left homeless by the war. Those Korean Americans who had come from North Korea were cut off from their families and were unable to return home. They remained exiles in America.

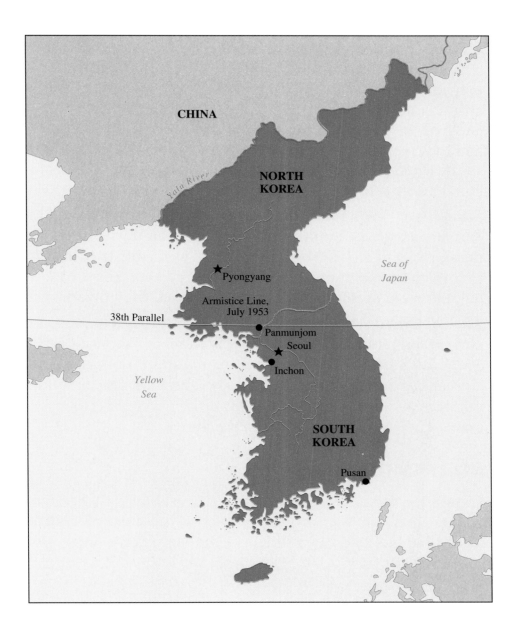

POSTWAR IMMIGRATION

War Brides   Many of the 40,000 American soldiers sent to Korea met and married Korean women. After World War II, Congress enacted laws allowing American soldiers to bring foreign "war brides" home with them. This law enabled the Americans sent to Korea to bring their Korean-born wives to America with them. Between 1951 and 1964, more than 28,000 Korean war brides immigrated to America.

The war brides were scattered all over America. They escaped from a war-torn and impoverished land, but they encountered problems in America. Since a large number married career soldiers, they were often found clustered around military bases. They were isolated from their families and from other Korean Americans. Many had little education, and they were not used to American culture. Some could not speak English or get jobs. Interracial couples were discriminated against. Many of the marriages ended in divorce.

Students   Also after the Korean War, about 10,000 South Korean students came to study in American universities. Of these, more than 7,500 remained. They were able to qualify to become permanent residents because they had skills or training that were useful to American businesses and universities.

The McCarran-Walter Act   In 1952, Congress passed a new immigration law called the McCarran-Walter Act. It ended all racial and ethnic bars to naturalization and gave Koreans an annual quota of 100. However, under the new law, relatives of citizens and permanent residents could also immigrate. They were not counted in the quota.

KOREAN ORPHANS

Soon after the Korean War ended, thousands of Americans adopted Korean War orphans. Many of these were children whose parents had been killed in the war. Some were also unwanted children who had been born to Korean women and American soldier fathers. No one knows how many orphans were brought to the United States. However, records show that 6,293 orphans were adopted through one adoption agency between 1955 and 1966.

The postwar adoptions were the beginning of a practice that still continues today. According to the U.S. Immigration and Naturalization Service, nearly 50,000 Korean orphans were adopted by Americans between 1978 and 1989.

Most Korean orphans come to the United States as infants. They learn English as their first language. Their American parents raise them completely as Americans. Although they look Asian, they may know little or nothing of their native land or culture.

Many Korean orphans have been adopted by Americans.

Immigration, 1965 to the Present

In 1965, Congress completely changed the immigration law. Under the new law, 120,000 people could immigrate to the United States each year from the Western Hemisphere. Another 170,000 could immigrate from the Eastern Hemisphere, including Europe and Asia. As many as 20,000 could immigrate from any one country. In addition, thousands of others could enter the United States under certain categories called "special preferences." These included parents, children, and spouses of American citizens and permanent residents. People who enter under the special-preference categories are not counted in the 20,000-person national limit. The new law was a great boon to Koreans. For the first time, they could enter the United States in large numbers. Now about 35,000 Koreans come each year.

Virtually all of the Korean immigrants come from South Korea. Some are refugees from North Korea who first moved to South Korea and then to the United States. Many South Koreans come to join family members. Others come to work in the United States. Some Koreans also came to escape political repression in South Korea. The Rhee government of South Korea and its successors were authoritarian. They allowed little political dissent. Only recently has the government instituted reforms and become more democratic.

TODAY'S IMMIGRANTS

In 1960, there were about 10,000 Korean Americans in the United States. Today there are between 800,000 and 1 million. Ninety percent have come since 1965 or were born here. The new immigrants who have come from Korea are very different from past immigrants. Many are women and children. Between 1959 and 1971, about 70 percent of Korean immigrants were women. Many were wives of U.S. citizens. Also since 1965, most Korean immigrants have been well-educated, middle-class Koreans. Between 15 and 25 percent of those arriving each year are professionals such as doctors, engineers, pharmacists, and nurses.

Although Korean immigrants live throughout the United States, about half live in the four states shown in the inset table below.

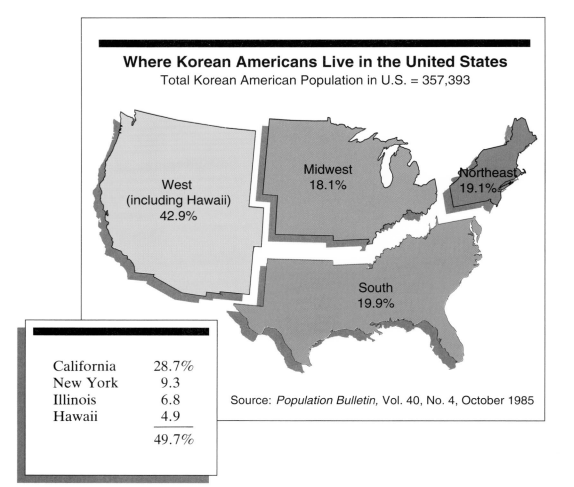

Where Korean Americans Live in the United States
Total Korean American Population in U.S. = 357,393

West (including Hawaii) 42.9%

Midwest 18.1%

Northeast 19.1%

South 19.9%

California	28.7%
New York	9.3
Illinois	6.8
Hawaii	4.9
	49.7%

Source: *Population Bulletin*, Vol. 40, No. 4, October 1985

Members of the Korean American Student Society at the University of California, Berkeley

KOREAN AMERICANS: A PROFILE

Most Korean Americans are city dwellers, well educated, and hardworking. After 1965, Koreans began arriving in numbers large enough to establish large Korean communities in many cities. More than 150,000 Korean Americans live in Los Angeles. Another 100,000 reside in New York City. Chicago also has a very large Korean American population.

Korean Americans are among the better-educated ethnic groups in America. Over 90 percent of men and about 70 percent of women are high school graduates. At least 40 percent of Korean Americans between the ages of twenty and twenty-four are enrolled in colleges or universities. Only about one-fourth of white Americans in the same age group are enrolled in college.

Korean Americans born in the United States work in the same occupations and professions as other Americans. A great many Korean Americans prefer to go into business for themselves. They usually run small businesses that employ family members and other Koreans. Recent immigrants are often forced to take low-paying jobs such as waiters or hospital orderlies.

PROBLEMS OF PROFESSIONALS

More than 13,000 Korean doctors, nurses, pharmacists, and dentists immigrated to the United States between 1965 and 1977. Several thousand more professionals have arrived since then. Korean medical and nursing schools annually produce many more doctors and other health-care professionals than the country can employ. A large number of those professionals choose to come to the United States. Once they arrive, they encounter several problems.

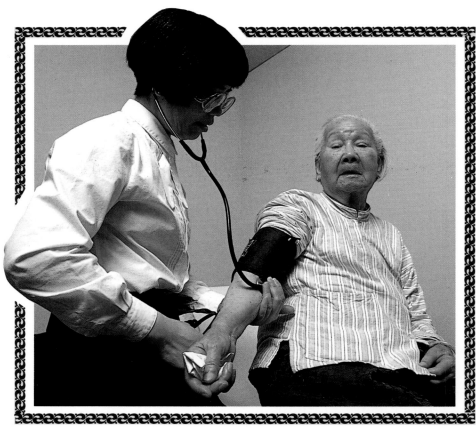

Many Korean American physicians work in inner-city or rural hospitals.

Newly arrived Korean professionals must learn English, if they don't already speak it. Then they must pass qualifying tests to obtain licenses to practice their professions. Often this involves returning to school for a period of time. In the meantime, they usually must take menial jobs.

Even when Korean American doctors qualify to practice medicine in the United States, they encounter discrimination. Most of them take jobs in inner-city or rural hospitals where other doctors do not want to work.

TODAY'S ENTREPRENEURS

A large percentage of Koreans know little or no English when they arrive in America. The language barrier prevents them from obtaining good jobs. This is one reason why Korean Americans go into business for themselves. Often, business owners need to learn only a few phrases of English to communicate with customers.

Some wealthy Korean businessmen and retired government officials arrive from Korea with large sums of money to invest in American businesses. Most Koreans, however, arrive with little or no money. Typically, newly arrived immigrants will start out as street vendors or work for other Koreans. During their first few years in the United States, the adult members of a Korean family all will work and pool their money to start a small business.

Many Korean Americans buy small fruit and vegetable stores. Koreans own about 1,000 of the 1,200 such enterprises in New York City. A large number of Korean Americans own liquor stores, wig shops, and dry cleaners.

Often Korean businesses are located in poor, high-crime areas of large cities. The owners risk robbery, shoplifting, even assault and murder to operate their businesses. Sometimes, the businesses barely make enough profit to survive. Some

Korean Americans own numerous small family-run businesses in New York City.

owners must keep their stores open sixteen to twenty-four hours a day. Usually family members work with no pay.

When a Korean American small business does succeed, the family is able to move to the suburbs, buy homes and cars, and enjoy a good life. Some successful Korean American business owners go on to buy bigger stores or to start chains of stores.

KOREAN AMERICAN WOMEN

For centuries in Korea, middle-class women could not go out in public in the daytime. They did not work, and most had household help. They lived with their in-laws and were expected to keep house, raise their children, and defer to their husbands in all things.

Life was—and is—very different in America for Korean women. The earliest immigrants had to work in the sugarcane fields right alongside the men, as only the peasant women at home had to work. Many of today's immigrant women also have to work in hard, menial jobs or in family-owned businesses. In addition, they must keep house and raise their children without the help of servants or a house full of in-laws.

As a result, Korean American women have become much more independent than they were at home in Korea. They have to make many decisions themselves. They are not so deferential to their husbands.

Some Korean American men believe that Korean American women have become too independent. Eligible bachelors often go back to Korea to shop for a bride who has not yet been "Americanized."

In 1973, Kim Hyung-Chan, a Korean American woman, wrote an article about the lives of Korean women in America. Here is part of that article:

Many Korean women in Korea carry the misconception that the women in America live in a "worldly heaven." To be sure, it is good for the wife to be out of the house of the in-laws and no longer subject to their domination, and assert her freedom as a woman as well as a wife and mother. However, these Korean women in Korea . . . are surprised when told there is a great deal of hardship that the Korean women go through here in this country.

Source: As quoted in Kim Hyung-Chan and Wayne Patterson, *The Koreans in America 1882–1974* (Dobbs Ferry, N.Y.: Oceana, 1974), pp. 122–123.

ILLEGAL IMMIGRANTS

In 1986, Congress adopted a new law (The Immigration Reform Act of 1986) to try to halt illegal immigration to the United States. An "amnesty" provision allowed illegal immigrants who came before 1982 to remain and become permanent residents. Those who came after 1982 can be deported to their home countries. Under the law, people who provide employment to illegal aliens may be fined. The law was aimed largely at the million or so Mexicans who have come to the United States illegally in recent years. It also applies to illegal immigrants from many other countries, including Korea.

There is a small but unknown number of Korean illegal aliens living in the United States. They usually go first to Mexico and hire guides, called *coyotes*, to smuggle them across the border. Then they go to Los Angeles or New York. Illegal—or undocumented—Korean aliens often get jobs working for other Korean Americans.

Some illegal Korean aliens have received amnesty. They are given "green cards," or permits that enable them to remain in America and get jobs. They must wait eighteen months to become permanent residents. Then they must wait another two to three years to bring their families over.

In recent years, the Korean Association of New York has arranged for more than 100 wives of former illegal Korean aliens to come to the United States for short visits. In some cases, the spouses have not seen each other in eight or nine years.

Gwang-Mee Pae, a New York supermarket manager, was an illegal alien. He has qualified for temporary residency. He hopes to bring his family over soon. He told the *New York Times* that he felt "in a state of danger" as an illegal alien. "Now I can walk down the street without being afraid when I see a police car."[1]

[1]*Source*: As quoted in the *New York Times*, April 15, 1989, p. 29.

NEIGHBORHOOD CONFLICTS

Many Korean immigrants have established businesses in poor sections of cities that are mainly inhabited by blacks. Blacks sometimes resent that these new immigrants are operating businesses in their neighborhoods. They feel that the Korean merchants are taking money out of the neighborhoods but not putting anything back in. Some blacks in New York and Philadelphia have organized boycotts of Korean stores.

The Korean store owners are only doing what nearly every other new immigrant group has done in years past. They start businesses in poor, inner-city neighborhoods where rents are lower but crime rates are high. Once they become prosperous, they move out, leaving the empty stores to newer immigrant groups. The Korean merchants need their black customers as much as blacks need neighborhood stores. Some Koreans are working with black leaders to find ways to overcome the conflicts.

Successful Korean American businesses have occasionally caused resentment in poor neighborhoods. Here police deal with a neighborhood boycott of a grocery store.

KOREAN AMERICANS TODAY

"Korea Town" The biggest concentration of Korean businesses, churches, and social centers in America lies along Olympic Boulevard just west of downtown Los Angeles. Korean immigrants have taken over a four-mile stretch of the boulevard and much of the surrounding area. The area is known as "Korea Town" or "Little Seoul," after the capital of South Korea. It boasts hundreds of Korean stores, plus hotels, restaurants, and offices. There are also dozens of Christian churches and many Buddhist temples.

Korea Town is the nerve center of southern California's 300,000 Korean immigrants. Korean Americans operate thirty-two newspapers, one twenty-four-hour radio station, and 150 associations to serve the Korean American community of southern California.

Olympic Boulevard, the heart of Los Angeles's Korea Town: the most diverse Asian American community in the United States

Associations   Many Korean Americans belong to small, informal groups made up of several families. These groups are like extended families. They are not based on kinship, but they help fill many of the same kinds of needs. For example, Korean Americans share special events such as christenings, weddings, and holidays with their family groups. These groups may be based on church membership, neighborhoods, sports, hobbies, or jobs. Korean Americans also belong to many other nizations:

Kyes   A *kye* is a revolving-credit association. A group of Koreans invests money in the kye. Then, one by one, each member can borrow from the kye to start a business or buy a home. Kyes have enabled thousands of Koreans to start their own businesses.

Alumni Associations   Many Koreans belong to alumni associations of the schools and colleges they attended in South Korea. Alumni associations are very popular among Korean Americans.

Business Associations   Korean Americans in the same industry often form associations to help one another with common problems. The Korean American Garment Industry Association is one example of this kind of group.

Political Associations   The Korean American community supports dozens of political organizations. Most of them are still focused on politics in Korea. However, the Korean American Political Association (KAPA) supports Korean candidates in local elections.

Professional Organizations   Each profession within the Korean American community has its own association. This includes artists, doctors, nurses, musicians, ministers, entertainers, and engineers. Many of these groups are concerned with helping members qualify for jobs in the United States.

KOREAN AMERICAN CHURCHES

There are about 2,000 Korean American churches in the United States. Nearly all of them are Protestant. Most Korean Catholics go to churches with mixed congregations. Most Korean American Protestants are Presbyterian or Baptist. More than 70 percent of all Korean Americans attend churches.

The modern churches fulfill the same role that the early Korean American churches did. In addition to providing spiritual guidance, they are the chief social center for their members. They sponsor Korean language schools for Korean American children. They also provide many social services for their members. They help Korean Americans deal with the government and social agencies. They help new immigrants find jobs and homes. They teach English to new arrivals. They provide family counseling. Some churches also organize lectures and seminars to help professionals qualify for jobs in America.

KOREAN AMERICAN MEDIA

Korean American newspapers help Koreans preserve their culture and identity. Korean Americans publish dozens of newspapers in Los Angeles and New York. The first Korean American newspaper was the *Korean News,* first published in Honolulu in 1905. The oldest Korean American newspaper still in existence is the *New Korea* (*Sinhan Minbo*). It began operations in 1907 in Oakland, California, as the *Mutual Cooperation News*. Later it moved to Los Angeles, where it is still published. Many Korean immigrants also subscribe to one of two large daily newspapers published in Korea. These newspapers, the *Hankook Ilbo* and the *Joong Ang Ilbo*, produce American editions in Los Angeles, New York, and Chicago.

Korean American newspapers inform immigrants of news from their homeland and important events and issues in America.

Korean American newspapers fulfill many roles. They provide information about the immigrants' homeland. They discuss issues that are important to Korean Americans and help form their opinions about those issues. They help unite the Korean American community. A typical Korean American newspaper may have articles about community events, weddings, Korean holiday celebrations, and news from South Korea. They also announce Korean cultural programs, such as concerts or operas.

In Los Angeles, some television stations broadcast programs in Korean for immigrants who enjoy programs in their mother tongue. These programs often discuss Korean politics and problems affecting Korean immigrants. Both Los Angeles and New York also have Korean-language radio stations that broadcast Korean music and public affairs programs.

KOREAN AMERICAN CULTURE

Korean immigrants usually quickly adopt American culture. Even in Korea, American clothing, goods, food, movies, and music are very popular. This is especially true for younger Koreans. Business people and government officials learn English because they believe it will help them get ahead in their careers. When they immigrate to the United States, many Koreans have already adopted an American life-style.

Korean Americans in Los Angeles and New York support Korean opera companies, symphony orchestras, dance troupes, writers, and artists. Most of these are concerned with the art of the Western world.

Many Koreans, however, try to keep alive some aspects of traditional Korean culture that are important to them. Korean language schools are available that teach folk songs and dances, as well as the language itself.

Korean Americans still observe some of the same holidays that they celebrated in Korea. Christmas, New Year's Day, and March 1 are their most important holidays. On March 1, 1919, a group of courageous Koreans tried to overthrow their Japanese masters. Even though the attempt failed, most Koreans regard that day as their independence day.

Korean Americans also hold special celebrations for a child's first birthday and for a family member's sixtieth birthday. In earlier times, life was so hard in Korea that many infants died during the first year of life. When babies did survive and reached their first birthday, they were welcomed into their family and society with a big party. The sixtieth birthday is also celebrated with a lavish party. In Korean tradition, people who live until their sixtieth birthday are considered to have lived out their full life span. After that day, they are entitled to the same kind of veneration that Koreans bestow on their ancestors.

DISTINGUISHED KOREAN AMERICANS

The Korean American community remained very small for most of this century. Nevertheless, it has produced several distinguished Korean Americans.

Philip Jaisohn (1866 – 1951)

Philip Jaisohn was one of the very first Koreans to come to America. He was born in Korea in 1866. He came to the United States as a student and political refugee in 1885.

Jaisohn studied medicine at George Washington University. He received his M.D. degree in 1895. After graduation, Dr. Jaisohn married a Caucasian woman. He returned to Korea in 1896 and started a newspaper and was expelled. He then started a medical practice in Philadelphia in 1898.

Dr. Jaisohn remained passionately interested in Korean independence all his life. After the March 1 independence movement failed in 1919, he formed an independence organization among Philadelphia Koreans. His group was named the First Korean Liberty Congress. After Korea was liberated in 1945, he returned for a brief visit. Jaisohn died at his home in Media, Pennsylvania, in 1951 at the age of eighty-four.

Syngman Rhee (1875 – 1965)

Syngman Rhee became the most important of the exiled independence movement leaders. He was born in Korea in 1875. As a young man, Rhee became very involved in independence politics. He was imprisoned from 1897 to 1904. After he was released, he came to the United States.

Rhee enrolled in George Washington University. After graduation, he earned postgraduate degrees in international relations: a master's degree from Harvard and a doctorate from Princeton. He returned to Korea briefly as a YMCA organizer, but he came back to the United States in 1912. In 1913, Rhee went to Hawaii to become principal of a school for Korean Americans. In Hawaii, he became a leader of the Korean American movement for Korean independence. In 1919, he was elected the first president of the Korean government in exile.

Rhee returned to Korea after its liberation in 1945. Three years later, he was elected its first president. Rhee's government gradually became more dictatorial and corrupt until Rhee was overthrown in 1960. He returned to exile in Hawaii, where he died in 1965.

Younghill Kang (1903 – 1972)

Younghill Kang came to America in 1921. He arrived nearly penniless, and he worked in a series of unskilled jobs. Despite his poverty, Kang was able to attend Harvard University and earn a degree in literature. He taught comparative literature at New York University and also worked for the Metropolitan Museum of Art in New York.

In 1931, Kang published an autobiographical novel about his life in Korea, *The Grass Roof.* In 1933, Kang won a Guggenheim Fellowship, which gave him the means to write another novel, *The Happy Grove.* Kang was the first Asian American to receive a Guggenheim. In 1937, he finished his last major novel, *East Goes West.* This book was about his trials as an Asian immigrant to America. Kang's novels were very popular in the 1930s. He was the first writer to share the Korean American experience with American readers.

Sammy Lee (1920 –)

Sammy Lee was born in California, the son of Korean immigrants. Lee's parents ran a chop suey restaurant. He graduated from Occidental College in 1943. Then he attended the University of Southern California (USC) School of Medicine. While at USC, Lee took up diving. He graduated from USC in 1947 and became a captain in the U.S. Army Medical Corps. The following year, he won the Gold Medal for platform diving and the Bronze Medal for springboard diving at the 1948 Olympics in London. He also won the Gold Medal for platform diving at the 1952 Olympics in Helsinki.

Despite his fame as an Olympic athlete, Dr. Lee suffered discrimination in his home state. In 1955, local realtors refused to sell him a home in Cedar Grove, California. He settled in Santa Ana, California, instead, and started a medical practice. Dr. Lee also ran a swimming and diving school there for many years. He still lives there today.

Kimchee, the national Korean dish

KOREAN CUISINE

Korean cooking is similar to that of Japan and China. Rice is the main staple in all three countries. Chinese, Japanese, and Korean cooks use many of the same basic ingredients and spices in their cooking. People in all three countries eat with chopsticks instead of knives and forks. Despite these similarities, Koreans do have their own distinct style of cooking. The climate is colder in the mountains of Korea than in Japan or many parts of China. Koreans like hot soups and very spicy foods. They use a lot of red pepper and garlic in their cooking.

Kimchee is the Korean national dish. It is such a staple of Korean cooking that it is served at every meal. Kimchee serves as a basic ingredient in many other Korean dishes as well. Kimchee can be made with celery, cabbage, cucumbers, or daikon, which is a large white Korean radish. In the fall, Korean housewives make enough kimchee to last through the winter. They combine the freshly harvested cabbage with onions, red peppers, garlic, sugar, water, and other ingredients. Then they place the kimchee in large crocks to ferment.

A Korean meal, featuring soup, rice, kimchee, and
stews

A typical Korean meal includes rice and kimchee, or other
vegetables. A Korean meal may also include a soup made of
soy sauce and beef, fish, or bean curd. Koreans also make
hearty stews of kimchee, meats, and a fiery red pepper paste.
The meal is eaten with chopsticks.

PROBLEMS OF KOREAN AMERICANS

Korean immigrants have adapted to American life very rapidly, but it has cost them dearly. Many Korean American families have comfortable incomes, nice homes, and many material possessions. But the Korean work ethic has caused stress and created severe problems in some families. Husbands and wives work sixteen to eighteen hours a day in family-owned businesses. Wives are also expected to take care of the home and children as well as work long hours on the job. These stresses have sometimes led to wife abuse, suicide, and divorce. In addition, some children left alone while parents work become involved in gangs, drugs, and juvenile delinquency.

Most Koreans came to America to give their children a good education and a better life. However, from the beginning, conflicts have existed between the immigrants and their children. Second-generation Korean Americans, born or educated in America, become Americanized very rapidly. They learn English faster than their parents. Often, the children are called on to translate for their parents. The second-generation children become very independent. They are not as respectful of their parents as children in Korea. They date and marry people from other ethnic groups. They become less interested in the Korean language or culture. These same conflicts occur between generations in all immigrant groups. American culture and education compel immigrant children to blend in with other Americans much faster than their parents. However, these generational differences are very painful to immigrant parents who remain faithful to the old ways.

TIES WITH THE HOMELAND

Most Korean Americans have maintained close ties with their homeland. The Korean Independence Movement in America lasted more than forty years until Korea was liberated in 1945.

Since the 1950s, the Korean War and the fact that their country is still divided have occupied Korean Americans.

Today's Korean Americans are still deeply concerned about events in their homeland. From the 1960s until recently, the South Korean government has been repressive. Meanwhile, North Korea remains a Communist dictatorship. Many Korean Americans hope that hostilities will soon end between North Korea and South Korea. They hope their country will be reunited.

It is not just politics that ties Korean Americans to Korea. Many still have family members there. Some Korean Americans make trips to Korea every few years to visit family and friends.

GOING HOME

After the Korean War, South Korea began to develop its industries. Today, it is one of the world's largest producers of automobiles, electronics, and ships. South Korea now exports hundreds of thousands of Hyundai cars to America and other countries each year. Hyundai, Gold Star, and Samsung compete with the United States and Japan to produce computer components, televisions, stereo equipment, and other electronic goods. Korean shipyards make most of the world's supertankers and freighters.

During the 1980s, Korea's economy grew dramatically. In addition, the recent democracy movement has brought about some political reforms. These factors have encouraged about 1,200 Korean Americans to return to Korea to live and work. Most of the returning Koreans are scientists and engineers who were educated in America.

The return of educated Korean Americans to their homeland has been a boon for Korea. However, it is hurting the United States. Many Asian Americans study science and

Hyundai car factory shipment, Ulsan, South Korea

engineering in college. American corporations count on employing them once they graduate. Not enough other Americans are interested in becoming scientists or engineers. Now, Korean Americans trained at American companies such as IBM and Honeywell have helped Korea catch up to the United States and Japan in the production of many goods.

For those returning to Korea, life is not as comfortable as it was in America. Housing is more crowded, and, for most people, the pay is less. Husbands work long hours and children go to school longer. American-born wives have to learn to be submissive in Korea's male-dominated society. Still, many Korean Americans want to return to Korea to help their homeland develop. Some are also homesick for family and friends in Korea.

THE FUTURE

Even though some Korean Americans are going back to Korea, most are staying in the United States. In addition, new immigrants continue to come to America at the rate of 35,000 each year. Census analysts expect the Korean American community to continue to grow through immigration and births. They estimate that the United States will have 1.3 million Korean Americans by the year 2000.

Second-generation Korean Americans are beginning to form families and have children. This third generation will become even more American. Korean Americans will follow the same path as older immigrant groups. They will lose their distinctive cultural traits. They will be aware of their backgrounds, but they will think of themselves primarily as Americans. English will be their chief language if not their only language. Their emphasis on education will ensure that their children will hold skilled jobs, move to the suburbs, and enjoy a thoroughly American life-style. They will come to hold the same values as other Americans. This same process has already Americanized English, Irish, Italian, Polish, and many other ethnic groups.

The future may change for North Korea and South Korea as well. If the cold-war thaw continues, the two countries may reunify into one country. This will enable families split by the Korean War to reunite. Some refugees living in the United States and other countries may be able to return home. As the economy improves in Korea, life will be better for Korean workers. Fewer Koreans will want to come to the United States, and more may decide to return home. The immigration flow will dwindle. Still, there will continue to be a large Korean population in the United States.

Women in traditional dress sewing costumes at a Korean National Day celebration in Golden Gate Park, San Francisco

Sources

Bouvier, Robert W., and Robert W. Gardner. "Immigration to the U.S.: The Unfinished Story." *Population Bulletin*, vol. 41, no. 4, November 1986. Washington, D.C.: Population Reference Bureau.

Gardner, Robert W., Bryant Robey, and Peter C. Smith. "Asian Americans: Growth, Change, and Diversity." *Population Bulletin*, vol. 40, no. 4, October 1985. Washington, D.C.: Population Reference Bureau.

Kim Hyung-Chan. *Dictionary of Asian American History*. New York: Greenwood, 1986.

Kim Hyung-Chan, and Wayne Patterson. *The Koreans in America, 1882–1974*. Dobbs Ferry, N.Y.: Oceana, 1974.

Kim, Illsoo. *New Urban Immigrants: The Korean Community in New York*. Princeton, N.J.: Princeton Univ. Press, 1981.

Kitano, Harry, H. L., and Roger Daniels. *Asian Americans: Emerging Minorities*. Englewood Cliffs, N.J.: Prentice-Hall, 1988.

Lee, Mary Paik. *Quiet Odyssey: A Pioneer Korean Woman in America*. Seattle: Univ. of Washington Press, 1990.

Melendy, H. Brett. *Asians in America: Filipinos, Koreans, and East Indians*. Boston: Twayne, 1977.

Takaki, Ronald. *Strangers from a Different Shore: A History of Asian Americans*. Boston: Little, Brown, 1989.

Index